北京风景集萃

Beijing in a Nutshell

Fifth edition 1994

ISBN 7-5052-0043-7
Copyright 1994 by the China Esperanto Press
Published by the China Esperanto Press, P.O.Box 77. Beijing, China
Distributed by China International Book Trading Corporation (Guoji Shudian)
35 W. Chegongzhuang Xiiu, Beijing, China
P. O. Box 399, Post code: 100044

北京風景集萃

Beijing in a Nutshell

Translated into English by Z. R. Xiong

中國世界語出版社出版　　北京

Published by the China Esperanto Press

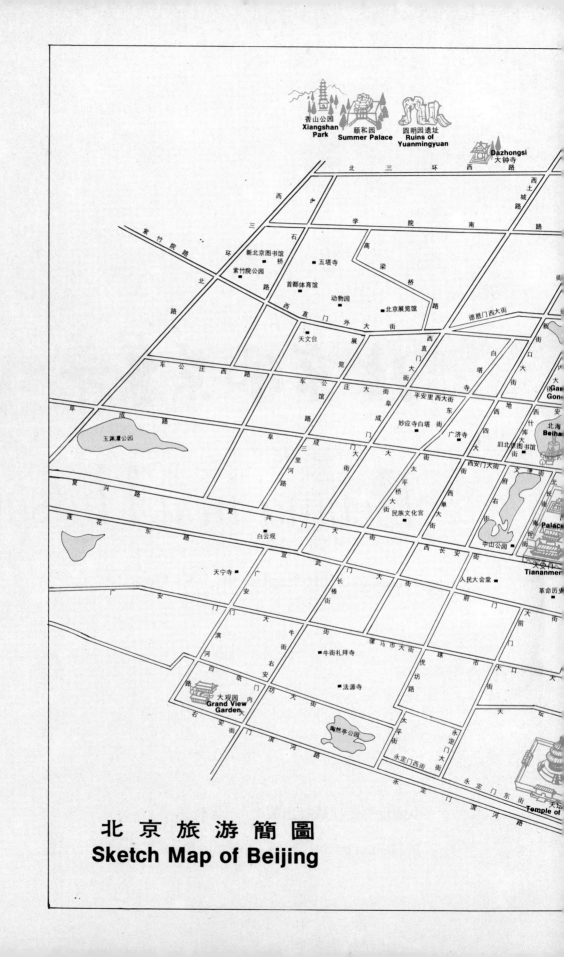

北 京 旅 游 簡 圖
Sketch Map of Beijing

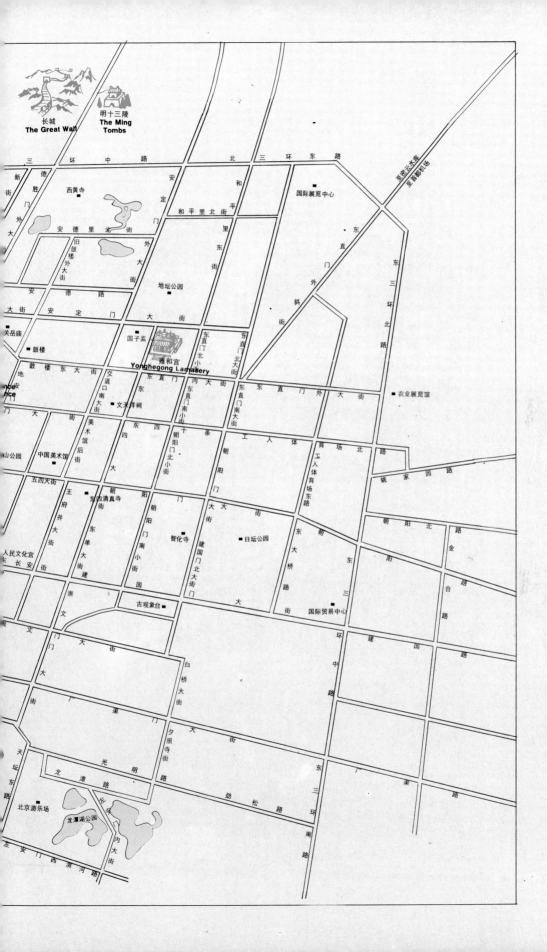

目　　録　CONTENTS

前　　言

北京是中華人民共和國的首都，世界歷史文化名城。

早在三千多年前，北京稱爲薊，是中國北方的一個重鎮。春秋（前 770-前 476 年）、戰國（前 475-前 221 年）時爲燕國國都。十世紀上半葉，遼代（公元 907-1125 年）定薊爲陪都，改名南京，又稱燕京。十二世紀中，金代（公元 1115-1234 年）正式建都於此，改稱中都。此後，歷代王朝亦在此建都。元代（公元 1271-1368 年）又把中都更名爲大都。直到一四○三年，明代（公元 1368-1644 年）開國皇帝朱元璋的四子朱棣當了皇帝後，把國都從現在的南京遷到這裏，才正式將大都定名爲北京。一九四九年十月一日，中華人民共和國成立，北京成爲首都和中國政治、經濟、交通、科學文化的中心。

北京地處華北平原北端，西北環山，東南爲平原。這種北依山險，南控平原的自然地勢，使它成爲歷代兵家必爭之地，又是貫通中國東北、華北地區的交通要衝。因其地勢重要，歷代王朝無不苦心經營，使之成爲世界上規模最大、歷史遺迹最多的名城之一。

這裏有世界上保存最完好、規模最宏大的皇宮——紫禁城，有風景絢麗、建築輝煌的皇家園林——頤和園、北海，有設計巧妙、氣勢恢弘的壇廟——天壇，還有工程浩大、蜿蜒萬里的古代軍事設施——長城，更有佈局嚴整、陵宇錯落的帝王陵寢——明十三陵……無論在蒼松翠柏間，在湖畔流水旁，還是在青山綠麓處，人們總可以找到自己流連忘返的古迹、勝景。

作爲旅遊勝地，每年到北京觀光的客人數以千萬計。人們不僅想飽覽北京的綽約風姿，還想買一本介紹北京的畫冊作紀念。爲了滿足旅遊者的需要，我們編輯出版了這本《北京風景集萃》。由於北京的名勝古迹實在太多，我們不可能逐一介紹。本書所舉景點只是它美麗風姿的縮影。願它能給您帶來方便和愉快。

Foreword

Beijing, the capital of the People's Republic of China, is a world-famous historical and cultural city.

Three thousand years ago Beijing was called Ji, an important town in northern China. During the Spring and Autumn and Warring States Periods (770-221 B.C.), it became the capital of the state of Yan. In the early tenth century the Liao Dynasty (907-1125) designated it its secondary capital, named Nanjing (Southern Capital), or Yanjing. In the middle of the twelfth century the Jin Dynasty (1115-1234) established their main capital at Yanjing and named it Zhongdu (Central Capital), after which many dynasties had their capital here. The Yuan Dynasty (1271-1368) changed Zhongdu to Dadu (Great Capital), until in 1403 Zhu Di, the fourth son of Zhu Yuanzhang, the founder of the Ming Dynasty (1368-1644), became the third emperor and transferred the court from Nanjing to here and renamed the city Beijing (Northern Capital). On October 1, 1949 the People's Republic of China was founded, and Beijing became its capital and political, economical, communications, scientific and cultural centre.

Beijing is located at the northern end of the vast North China Plain, on the northwest surrounded by mountains and on the southeast by plains. Its geographical setting of mountains to the north and plains to the south has made it a place contested by the strategists of past dynasties and a modern communications hub of Northeast and North China. Indeed it is because of its important topography that all dynasties took great pains to develop the place, turning it into one of the world's largest cities and one of the best endowed with historical remains.

Beijing has the world's largest well-preserved imperial palace — the Forbidden City; beautiful, magnificent imperial parks such as the Summer Palace and Beihai Park; huge, well-designed temples like the Temple of Heaven; the huge five-thousand-kilometre-long military project of the Great Wall; the superbly-constructed necropolis of the Ming Tombs — anywhere you go in Beijing, whether under ancient pine and cypress trees, on the banks of the lakes and rivers or into the green hills and mountains, you can find historical sites and scenic spots whose attractions are quite beguiling.

Beijing is an excellent place for tourists. Tens of millions of visitors come to Beijing every year. In addition to enjoying the captivating beauty of the ancient yet modern city, they would appreciate an album to keep their memory of it fresh or to give to friends as a souvenir to let them share what they have seen in Beijing.

For them we have compiled this album. But Beijing's historical sites and scenic spots are too numerous for us to have included all of them. What you see here is but an epitome, which we hope will serve as a guide and help and please you and your friends.

天 安 門

Tiananmen

原爲明清兩代皇城的正門，位於北京市中心。天安門始建於一四一七年，稱承天門，一六五一年重修，改名天安門。在高大的紅色城墻上開有五個拱形門，城臺上有九開間的重檐城樓，紅柱黃瓦，巍峨壯麗。前後各立華表一對，門前有金水河，跨河有漢白玉石橋五座。橋前爲天安門廣場。一九四九年十月一日，毛澤東主席在天安門城樓上宣告中華人民共和國成立。

Tiananmen (Gate of Heavenly Peace) is located in the heart of Beijing. The main gate to the Imperial City of the Ming and Qing Dynasties, it was first erected in 1417 and known as Chengtianmen (Gate for Receiving Orders from Heaven). In 1651 it was rebuilt and given its present name. The gate itself consists of a red platform with five vaulted gateways, surmounted by a wooden gate-tower. The magnificent gate-tower has a double roof of yellow glazed tiles and vermilion columns. Before and behind the gateways are two pairs of white marble columns. In front of Tiananmen is the Gold Water River with five white marble bridges crossing it. Further ahead, in front of the bridges is Tiananmen Square. The late Chairman Mao Zedong proclaimed the founding of the People's Republic of China from the rostrum of Tiananmen on October 1, 1949.

鳥瞰天安門廣場　這是北京的中心廣場，面積爲四十公頃，是世界上最大的廣場。北側屹立着天安門，中央爲人民英雄紀念碑，碑南是毛主席紀念堂和正陽門，東西兩側有中國歷史博物館、中國革命博物館和人民大會堂。廣場佈局嚴整，氣勢宏偉。

A bird's-eye view of Tiananmen Square

The heart of Beijing, the square covers an area of 40 hectares, the largest in the world. Around the square are many ancient and modern buildings: Tiananmen Gate-tower to the north, the Monument to the People's Heroes in the centre, the Chairman Mao Zedong Memorial Hall and Zhengyangmen to the south, the Museum of the Chinese Revolution and the Museum of Chinese History to the east, and the Great Hall of the People to the west. Well arranged, the square is very magnificent.

節日之夜的人民大會堂

The Great Hall of the People on a festival night

天安門前的華表

The White Marble Column

The Palace Museum

　　舊稱紫禁城，是明清兩代的皇宮，先後有二十四個皇帝在這裏居住過。始建於一四〇六——一四二〇年，後經多次重建。故宮佔地七十二公頃，共有房屋九千餘間，周圍設十多米高的宮墻和五十多米寬的護城河，宮墻四隅有角樓。故宮主要建築分外朝和內廷兩大部分。外朝以太和、中和、保和三大殿為主體，建在三層漢白玉石臺基上，是皇帝行使權力、舉行隆重典禮的地方；內廷以乾清宮、交泰殿、坤寧宮為主體，是皇帝處理朝政和居住的地方，其兩側東、西六宮為妃嬪的住所。故宮是中國現存規模最大、最完整的宮殿建築羣。整個建築按中軸綫對稱佈局，主體突出，層次分明，體現了中國建築藝術的優秀傳統和獨特風格。故宮珍藏有大量歷史文物和珍貴藝術品，也是中國最大的文化藝術博物館。

The Palace Museum, also known as the Purple Forbidden City, was the palace of the Ming and Qing Dynasties. Twenty-four emperors lived here over a span of more than 491 years. Constructed in the years from 1406 to 1420 and rebuilt many times later, the Imperial Palace covers an area of 72 hectares, with more than 9,000 buildings within it. Around it is a battlemented wall ten metres high, and outside the wall is a moat 50 metres wide. At each corner of the wall is a three-storeyed watch-tower. The main palace buildings are divided into two parts: the outer court and the inner court. The outer court has three main halls standing on a three-tiered, balustraded terrace of white marble: Taihedian (Hall of Supreme Harmony), Zhonghedian (Hall of Central Harmony) and Baohedian (Hall of Preserved Harmony). They are the places where the emperor received high officials and conducted the administration of the empire. The inner court includes Qianqinggong (Palace of Celestial Purity), Jiaotaidian (Hall of Celestial and Terrestrial Union), Kunninggong (Palace of Terrestrial Tranquillity). These are the places where the emperor lived and conducted day-to-day administration. On either side of the three central palaces are the twelve courtyards that were once inhabited by concubines, dowagers and maids. The Palace Museum is the largest and most complete group of palace buildings existing in China today. Laid out in a strict symmetry, the buildings embody the fine tradition and unique style of ancient Chinese architectural art. With its magnificent halls and courtyards and its imperial collection of arts and antiques, the whole palace is now a museum of world importance for Chinese history, culture and art.

故　宮　The Palace Museum

午門　故宮正門。城臺上有九開間的大型門樓，左右各有方亭兩座，樓亭巍峨，莊嚴宏偉。

Wumen (Meridian Gate), the main and south gate to the palace. On its red platform is a nine-bay wide gate-tower with two square pavilions on either side.

神武門　故宮北門。門樓上原有鐘鼓，黃昏後鳴鐘一百零八聲，隨後起更敲鼓，至拂曉復鳴鼓。清代選秀女，應選女子進出此門。

Shenwumen (Gate of Divine Might), the north gate to the palace. The gate-tower originally contained drums and bells. Every day at dusk, the bells would toll 108 times. After that the drums would beat to tell the hour at each watch of the night until again the bell sounded at sunrise. During the Qing Dynasty the court often chose beautiful maids, and the chosen girls would pass this gate when they were sent to the palace.

遠眺角樓　故宮四隅各設一座角樓，樓爲三重檐，全部木結構，樓頂用七十二條脊銜接，縱橫交錯，外形奇特，是中國古建築的傑作。

Watchtower viewed from the distance. At each corner of the Forbidden City wall is a three-storeyed watchtower exquisitely constructed of wood with triple eaves and 72 ridges. They are masterpieces of ancient Chinese architecture.

角樓近景　The watchtower

太和殿内景
Inside Taihedian

太和殿　俗稱"金鑾殿"，是明清兩代皇帝即位、節日慶賀和朝會大典的地方。

Taihedian (Hall of Supreme Harmony), or Throne Hall. During the Ming and Qing Dynasties the emperor ascended the throne, received high officials, celebrated important festivals and held grand ceremonies here.

①太和殿寶座靠背上的龍頭
②寶座扶手
③寶座靠背
④寶座底座

A. Dragon's head on the back of the throne
B. Handrail of the throne
C. Back of the throne
D. Pedestal of the throne

中和殿　皇帝在太和殿舉行盛典前略事休息的地方。

Zhonghedian (Hall of Central Harmony). This was the place where the emperor held rehearsals for ceremonies.

中和殿內的肩輿

Sedan-chair in
Zhonghedian

雕石御路　位於保和殿後，御路長十六點五七米，寬三點零七米，厚一點七米，重約二百噸。它是用一整塊艾葉青石料雕成的，是石雕藝術中的瑰寶。

The carved-marble imperial ramp.　Located behind Baohedian, the ramp consists of a 16.57 metre-long, 3.07 metre-wide and 1.7 metre-thick white marble slab weighing more than 200 tons, carved with a dragon flying amid clouds.

乾清宫　明代帝、后的寝宫；清代除做寝宫外，亦做临朝听政和接见外国使臣之用。乾清宫、交泰殿和坤宁宫合称后三宫，与外朝三大殿构成故宫的核心。

Qianqinggong (Palace of Celestial Purity). This was the emperor's bedroom, but was also used for day-to-day administration and meeting foreign envoys.

乾清宫内景　**Inside Qianqinggong**

交泰殿和坤宁宫　Jiaotaidian and Kunninggong

坤宁宫皇帝大婚洞房　　The emperor's bridal chamber in Kunninggong

储秀宫　是内廷东、西六宫之一。慈禧太后五十岁时耗巨资翻修一新，并在此居住过十年。

Chuxiugong (Palace for Gathering Elegance). When Empress Dowager Cixi was fifty she spent a large amount of money rebuilding this hall in the inner court. She lived here for ten years.

御花園千秋亭　故宮中共有四處花園：御花園、建福宮花
園、慈寧宮花園和寧壽宮花園。御花園中的殿宇和樹石，均爲十
五世紀的遺物，千秋亭和萬壽亭是對稱的兩座建築。

Qianqiu Pavilion in Yuhuayuan (Imperial Garden). In the Imperial Palace
there are four gardens: Yuhuayuan, Jianfugong, Cininggong and Ningshougong. The pavilions, towers, trees and rocks in the garden all are left from the
fifteenth century. The Qianqiu Pavilion and Wanshou Pavilion are two spots
of captivating beauty.

堆秀山　山上的御景亭是帝、后重陽登高觀景的地方。

Duixiushan (Hill of Accumulated Elegance). The Yujing Pavilion on the hill was the place where the emperor and empress ascended to enjoy a distant view on the Double Ninth Festival.

寧壽宮花園中的流杯渠　渠作如意形回繞，引水於渠中，杯浮水上，飲酒咏詩，其樂無窮，有"曲水流觴"之説。

The Flowing-Cup Channel in Ningshougong Garden. The small channel runs like an "S". Water was led into the channel allowing for cups to be floated upon it. While watching the scene, people would drink wine and compose poems. From this game sprang happiness and glee beyond words. Thus the saying, "On winding water flows the cup."

聳秀亭雪景　亭前爲數丈峭壁，若由下上仰，可見"一綫天"奇景。

Songxiu Pavilion in the snow. Before the pavilion is a cliff several leagues high. Looking up from the bottom, one can see the marvellous scene "One Thread Sky".

珍妃井　清末，光緒皇帝寵愛的珍妃被慈禧太后令太監推入此井而死，故此得名。

Zhenfei Well. At the end of the Qing Dynasty Emperor Guangxu's beloved concubine, Zhenfei, was pushed into this well by eunuchs acting on orders of Empress Dowager Cixi. So the well takes the concubine's name.

北 海 公 園
Beihai Park

位於故宮西北角。早在公元十世紀，遼代就在這裏始建行宮。金代繼遼代以後挖海壘島，並用大批太湖石堆砌假山，起殿築閣，立坊造欄，建成一座離宮。元代三次擴修瓊華島，並以此爲中心，建成大都城；明代亦大興土木，在湖濱修了五龍亭。到了清代乾隆（公元 1736-1796）年間，這裏連續施工三十年，一座規模宏大、設計精巧的皇家園林終臻完美。

北海由團城、瓊華島、東岸景區和西岸景區組成。瓊華島是全園中心，它通過渡船和石橋與其他景區連成一個整體。北海置景獨特，建築精美，是北京著名的旅遊勝地。

Beihai Park is located at the northwest corner of the Palace Museum. As early as the 10th century a secondary imperial palace was begun under the Liao Dynasty. In the Jin Dynasty a lake was dug, Qionghuadao (Jade Flower Island) was built up with an artificial hill made of rocks from Lake Tai, and many halls, pavilions and archways were constructed. The place became the Jin secondary palace. In the Yuan Dynasty Qionghuadao was rebuilt three times and became the centre of its capital Dadu (Great Capital). The Ming Dynasty saw more construction and renovation; Wulongting (Five Dragon Pavilions) on the north bank of Beihai Lake dates from then. During the Qianlong reign (1736-1796) of the Qing Dynasty, large-scale construction took place and lasted 30 years. By then a large, exquisite imperial garden was finally completed.

Beihai Park consists of Tuancheng (Round City), Qionghuadao (Jade Flower Island) and Scenic Spots on the Western and Eastern Banks. Qionghuadao, the centre of the park, is joined to other parts of the park via the stone bridges and the ferry. With wonderful sceneries and exquisite buildings, Beihai Park is a very famous Beijing park.

北　　海
Beihai Park

北海水上蛟龍　**Dragons.**

白塔　位於瓊華島之巔，建於一六
五一 年， 塔高三十五點九米，通身潔
白，是北海 的標誌。

The White Dagoba. Located at the top of
Qionghuadao and built in 1651, the 35.9-metre-
high dagoba is the symbol of Beihai Park.

善因殿　位於白塔前，爲仿木琉璃結構，上圓下方，頂爲銅質筒瓦，鎦金寶頂。方形殿的四周墻壁鑲嵌着四百四十五尊琉璃佛像。

Shanyindian. Located in front of the White Dagoba, it is a glazed building of unique style, with a roof of bronze tube-like tiles and a gold-plated pinnacle. On its four walls are inlaid 445 glazed statues of Buddhas.

静心齋　北海的園中之園。佈局緊凑、玲瓏，遊人置身園中，步移景現，變化無窮。

Jingxingzhai (Tranquil Heart Studio). Known as "a garden within a garden", it is a uniquely quiet place with elegant buildings. In the past the emperor used to study here.

畫舫齋　北海的又一處園中之園，亭榭圍合，游
廊連接，池中游魚嬉戲，青萍浮動，極富詩情畫意。

Huafangzhai. Another garden within a garden, the courtyard is a most intriguing building, which combines the architectural characteristics of the northern Chinese courtyard with
the style of the southern Chinese garden. With fish swimming
among the drifting duckweed, the place is very picturesque and
poetic.

瓊島春陰　碑上題字爲乾隆皇帝御書，原爲燕京八景之一。
這裏古木參天，濃蔭蔽日，環境極爲幽靜。

Qiongdaochunyin (Jade Islet in Shady Springtime). The inscription on the tablet was written by Emperor Qianlong. Originally known as one of the Eight Views of Yanjing, it is a quiet place with ancient trees reaching to the sky.

延樓游廊　游人漫步游廊，南眺白塔，北望碧海，仿佛置身江南。

Yanlou Corridor. Walking along the corridor, visitors can enjoy scenes of the White Dagoba on the southern side and the vast lake on the northern side.

銅仙承露盤　建於十八世紀，用來承接露水，爲帝后拌藥用，旨在延年益壽。

The Bronze Statue Holding a Plate to Collect Dew. It was cast in the eighteenth century to collect the dew from heaven to take medicine with, in order to prolong life.

西岸景區　遠眺五亭，宛若遊龍戲水，故名五龍亭。

The scenic spots on the western bank of Beihai Lake. The Five Dragon Pavilions viewed from the distance are constructed to look like a dragon sporting in the water.

五龍亭　原是帝、后垂釣、賞月和觀煙火的地方。

The Five Dragon Pavilions. This is the place where emperors and empresses used to come fishing, enjoy the moon or watch fireworks.

　　團城　是一座高六米的圓形城臺，臺上古木扶
疏，殿亭華麗，廊廡曲折，是一處精緻的小園林。

　　Tuancheng (Round City). Located on a 6-metre high
fortress with crenels along its walls, it is an exquisite small
garden with many magnificent buildings, ancient trees and
winding corridors.

承光殿　是團城上的主要建築物，呈重檐歇山正
方形，四方各推出單檐卷棚式抱廈一間，造型別具一
格，極富觀賞價值。

Chengguangdian (Hall for Receiving the Light). The main
building within the Round City, the square hall has a double-
eaved roof in a unique style.

承光殿玉佛　爲一整塊白玉石雕成，通身潔白，光澤清潤，袈裟上鑲嵌寶石，至爲珍貴。

The Jade Statue of Buddha inside Chengguangdian. Carved from a single piece of lustrous white jade, this priceless statue is a flawless work beautifully inlaid with gems.

團城白皮古松。

Lacebark pine tree in the Round City

　　九龍壁　壁兩面各有九條琉璃蟠龍戲珠於波濤雲海之中，形象生動，絢麗多彩，使人嘆爲觀止。

The Nine-dragon Screen. The screen is 5 metres high, 27 metres long and 1.2 metres thick, depicting nine dragons sporting with pearls among billowing waves. It is both colourful and magnificent.

玉瓮　係墨玉琢成，是六百多年前的遺物，曾流失，一七四九年被找回，置於玉瓮亭。玉瓮雕刻精美，是石雕藝術中的珍品。

Jade Bowl. Carved out of a single piece of black jade, the bowl is more than 600 years old. It was once lost but found again in 1749 and put in a pavilion especially built for it. It is an exquisite piece of art.

頤 和 園

Yiheyuan

　　位於北京西北郊，原名清漪園，是清代皇家花園和行宮。面積二百九十公項，是中國現存規模最大的園林之一。一八六○年被英法聯軍焚毀，一八八八年慈禧太后挪用海軍經費五百萬兩白銀重建，歷時十年，竣工後改名頤和園。

　　頤和園北依萬壽山，南抱昆明湖，其間點綴着殿堂樓閣，水榭亭橋。全園佈局精妙，以佛香閣爲主體，充分利用地形和水面，從假山的堆造到曲徑的走向，從樓閣的配置到花木的點綴，從堤埂的壘砌到橋樑的造型，無不表現了相得益彰的整體園林藝術效果。"雖由人造，宛自天成"。它以特有的魅力享譽海內外。

Yiheyuan, known to the world as the Summer Palace, was an imperial park of the Qing Dynasty. Located in the northwestern outskirts of Beijing, it occupies 290 hectares and is one of China's largest parks. In 1860 an Anglo-French joint force invaded Beijing and burnt it down. In 1888 Empress Dowager Cixi diverted 5,000,000 taels of silver earmarked for the navy to restore the park. The restoration took nearly 10 years, and after that the park was changed to its present name.

The park's main features are Wanshoushan (Longevity Hill) and Kunminghu (Kunming Lake). Its natural beauty is set off by a multitude of highly decorative halls, towers, galleries, pavilions, kiosks and bridges. Especially noteworthy is the ingenious way in which the architects adapted the buildings to blend in with or accentuate the natural surroundings. With its special charms, the park is famed both at home and abroad.

頤　和　園　Yiheyuan

　　佛香閣　連同臺基高六十一米，八面
三層四重檐，巍峨壯麗，是頤和園的標
誌。

Foxiangge (Tower of Buddhist Incense). Sixty-
one metres high including the base, this octagonal
tower has three storeys with double eaves and a
round roof of glazed tiles. It is the park's main
attraction and also its symbol.

　　昆明湖　面積有二百多公頃，湖中有知春亭、長堤、十七孔橋和龍王廟等勝景。

　　Kunminghu (Kunming Lake). Covering an area of more than 200 hectares, the lake has many scenic spots such as Zhichunting, the Long Causeway, the Seventeen-Arch Bridge and the Dragon-King Temple.

仁壽殿　清代帝、后處理朝
政的地方，其陳設一如當年臨朝
狀。

Renshoudian (Hall of Benevolent
Longevity). This is the place where the
Empress Dowager and Emperor Guang-
xu conducted the affairs of state.

德和園大戲樓　高二十一
米，三層均可演出。慈禧太后嗜
戲成癖，耗銀七十萬兩建造此
樓。它是中國現存最大的古戲
樓。

Deheyuan Theatre. This 21-metre
high three-storeyed theatre was built
especially for Empress Dowager Cixi on
her sixtieth birthday, and its construction cost over 700,000 taels of silver. It
is the largest ancient theatre existing in
China.

長廊　全長七百二十八米，枋樑上繪彩圖八千餘幅，取材爲
花鳥蟲魚、民間傳説和古典小説。

The Long Corridor. This covered walkway is 728 metres long, and on its
beams are painted over 8,000 paintings of birds, flowers and human figures
from legends, folk tales and classical novels.

畫中游　登閣憑眺，每窗一景，慈禧和后妃們常在此憩息和飲宴。

Huazhongyou (Pavilion of Wandering in Pictures). Each window of the pavilion produces a different view. Walking in the corridor is like wandering in pictures. The Empress Dowager used to rest or sup here.

衆香界　造型別致，裝飾華麗，是座宗教牌坊。

Zhongxiangjie (Archway of Buddhist Incense). This is a magnificent Buddhist archway.

　　五方閣　建在高大的臺基上，亭閣錯落、林木扶疏，是頤和園主要景點之一。

Wufangge (Pentagonal Pavilion). Constructed on a huge stone plinth in a unique style, the pavilion is a famous scenic spot.

寶雲閣　又叫銅亭，通體呈蟹青冷古銅色，重二十點二萬公斤，是世界上罕見的銅質建築物。

Baoyunge (Precious Cloud Pavilion). This kiosk made entirely of bronze weighs 202,000 kilogrammes. There are few bronze buildings like it in the world.

慈禧太后像　一九〇五年，荷蘭畫家華士·胡博（Hubert VOS）應聘爲慈禧畫像，成像後陳列於排雲殿。

Portrait of Empress Dowager Cixi. This large oil-painting of the Empress Dowager was presented to her by the Dutch painter Hubert Vos in 1905. It is displayed in Paiyundian.

諸趣園　園內亭堂樓榭繞池而建，佈局嚴謹，小巧玲瓏，極具蘇州園林風格，被稱爲園中之園。

Xiequyuan (Garden of Harmonious Interests). Built around a lotus covered pond in the style of Suzhou gardens, the exquisite towers and pavilions are connected by a long gallery. It is known as the Garden Within a Garden.

排雲殿內景　此殿背靠萬壽山，金碧輝煌，是羣臣爲慈禧祝壽的地方。殿內陳設如初，各種寶物多是朝賀的貢品。

Paiyundian (Hall of Dispelling the Clouds). This magnificent hall is the place where the Empress Dowager used to celebrate her birthday, and most of the objects on display are gifts from high officials.

清晏舫　因船體用巨大條石建成，又叫"石舫"，取"水能載舟，亦能覆舟"典故，寓意清王朝堅如磐石，水不能覆。

Qingyanfang (Boat for Pure Banquets). Also known as the Marble Boat, it has two decks built from large stone blocks, stained glass windows, and elaborately carved marble facing.

知春亭　四面環水，亭畔點綴山石，種植桃柳。冬去春來，湖冰最早在這裏消融，告知人們，春天已經來臨。

Zhichunting (Tower of Perceiving the Spring). Surrounded by water, the tower stands among rocks and peach and willow trees. Every year the frozen lake begins to melt here first, telling the arrival of spring.

玉帶橋　拱高而薄，橋身、橋欄用青白石和漢白玉石雕砌，呈曲綫形，宛如玉帶。

Yudaiqiao (Jade Belt Bridge). The graceful fully-bowed bridge built from white marble looks like a jade belt.

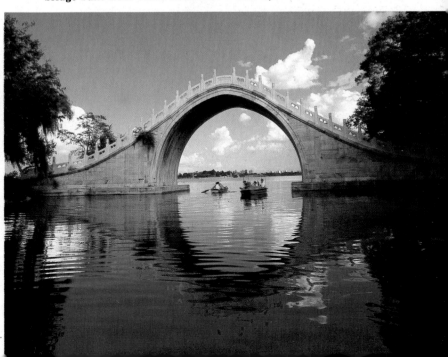

十七孔橋　長一百五十米，寬七米，橋欄望柱上雕有五百四十四隻大小不同的獅子。

The Seventeen-Arch Bridge. This bridge is 150 metres long and 7 metres wide, the largest stone bridge in the park. It has 544 stone lions of different sizes carved on its pillars.

銅牛　牛背上鑄有篆體銘文，形象逼真，素有"神牛"之稱。

Bronze Ox. Its back casted with inscriptions, the lifelike animal is known as "Divine Ox".

四大部洲　建於萬壽山後，典型的西藏
桑鳶寺式的宗教建築，曾毀於戰火。這是修
復後的壯景。

At the back of Wanshoushan is a massive
complex of buildings forming a Tibetan-style temple. It was devastated in wars. This is the restored
temple.

香嚴宗印之閣　象徵佛教中的須彌山。

This temple symbolizes Sumeru.

頤和園後湖　這裏幽雅靜謐，湖岸垂柳倒映，野花自開自落，富有江南水鄉情趣。

The Back Lake. The Back Lake of Yiheyuan is quiet and tastefully laid out. With hanging willows and wild flowers on its banks, it looks like a landscape of south China.

天　壇
Tiantan

　　明清兩代帝王祭天的場所。據史載，郊祀天地，周代（前 11 世紀-前 256 年）已成大典，漢（前 206-公元 220 年）、唐（公元 618-907 年）以後，相沿成制。十五世紀初，明代建成天地壇，合祭天地，中葉實行四郊分祀天地日月之制，此處專供祭天，更名天壇。清代（公元 1644-1911 年）予以擴建，成爲中國現存最大的一座壇廟建築。

　　天壇佔地二百七十三公頃，由兩道壇牆構成內壇、外壇，主要建築物集中在南北兩端，中間由一條長三百六十米的條石臺基相連。由南至北分別爲圜丘、皇穹宇、祈年殿和齋宮等。整個天壇設計精巧，色彩調和，建築藝術高超，是中國最出色的古建築之一。

Tiantan (Temple of Heaven) is the place where the emperors of the Ming and Qing Dynasties used to offer sacrifices to heaven. According to historical records, the worship of heaven in the suburbs began in the Zhou Dynasty (11th century-256 B.C.) and became a rule in the Han Dynasty (206 B.C.-A.D. 220) and the Tang Dynasty (618-907 A.D.). In the early 15th century the Ming Dynasty began to build an altar to offer sacrifices to heaven and earth together and in the middle of the 15th century they built altars at four different places to worship the heaven, the earth, the sun and the moon separately. This altar was constructed specifically for the worship of heaven in the Ming. It was enlarged in the Qing (1644-1911). Now Tiantan is the largest group of temple buildings in China.

Tiantan covers an area of 273 hectares, and is enclosed by a double wall. The main temple buildings are clustered at the northern and southern ends of a long central causeway, 360 metres long. The main buildings include Huanqiu (Circular Mound), Huangqiongyu (Imperial Vault of Heaven), Qiniandian (Hall of Prayer for Good Harvest) and Zhaigong (Abstinence Palace). The whole of Tiantan displays elegant design, superb craft and harmonious use of colour. It is one of China's most outstanding ancient architectural creations.

天　壇　Tiantan

齋宮　又稱無樑殿，是天壇內一組龐大的建築物。宮四周有高墻環繞，高墻內外有護城河和侍衛住房數百間，宮內還有正殿、典守房和鐘樓等建築。皇帝祭天前，需沐浴齋戒三天，並在典禮前一天進入天壇，下榻齋宮。

Zhaigong (Abstinence Palace).　Zhaigong, also known as the Beamless Palace, is a group of huge buildings in Tiantan. Inside and outside its surrounding walls there are moats and several hundred houses for guards. Inside the palace are the main hall, living quarters, bell tower and many other buildings. Before the emperor came to offer sacrifices to heaven, he would wash and commence a three-day fast, and on the day before the ceremony was held, he would come to Tiantan and stay in this palace.

齋宮裏的寢宮內景
The interior of the Abstinence Palace.

齋宮裏的鐘樓

The bell tower in the
Abstinence Palace.

62

丹陛橋　是連接祈年殿、皇穹宇和圜丘的漢白玉石長橋，表示從人間至天上的路途遙遠。

Danbiqiao (Cinnabar Stairway Bridge). This long causeway is built from white marble. It represents the distant journey between the human world and heaven.

具服臺　是皇帝祭天時整理服具的地方。

Jufutai (Terrace for Hanging Clothes). This is the place where the emperor rectified his clothes for the sacrifice.

祈年殿　是明清兩代皇帝祈禱皇天賜福、五穀豐登的場所。大殿採用中國傳統的木結構體系，造型奇特，結構精巧，具有很高的藝術價值。

Qiniandian (Hall of Prayer for Good Harvest). This is the place where the emperors of the Ming and Qing Dynasties prayed in person for good harvests every year. The hall is a circular wooden structure with a unique architectural style.

七十二長廊　是祭天時運送祭品的必經之路。長廊原來前有窗，後有墻，又稱"七十二連房"。

The Long Gallery. Also known as the Seventy-two Connected Houses, this gallery was the way for delivering sacrifices.

祈年殿神位

The shrine in Qiniandian.

祈年殿藻井　The caisson ceiling of Qiniandian.

皇穹宇 是儲存"皇天上帝"牌位的大殿。祭天時把牌位取
出，放在圜丘上祭祀，祭天後再放回原處。

Huangqiongyu (Imperial Vault of Heaven). Its function was to house
the memorial tablet of the "Supreme Ruler of Heaven". The memorial
tablet would be taken out before the emperor came to pray and sent back
when the praying was over.

皇穹宇外門　Outside Huangqiongyu.

　　回音壁　　是圓形磨磚對縫的圍墻。若兩人分別站在東西墻根，一人對墻低聲說話，聲波沿着墻壁連續反射前進，另一人可以清晰聽見。

　　The Echo Wall. It was built according to the principle that a sound wave bounces off a curved wall many times in succession. A whisper at one point of the wall can be heard clearly at an opposite point.

　　圜丘　又稱"祭天臺"，是皇帝冬至日（公歷大約在每年 12 月 22 日前後，此日太陽幾乎直射南回歸綫）祭天的地方。中國古人以天爲陽，因此圜丘的壇面、臺階、欄杆等所用的石塊，欄板的尺度和數目都用最大的陽數（奇數），即九或九的倍數。

Huanqiu (Circular Mound). Every year at the time of the winter solstice (around December 22), the emperor came here personally to offer sacrifices to heaven. According to ancient Chinese cosmology, the sun is a manifestation of the yang (male) principle. Therefore the figures and dimensions of the surface of Huanqiu, its steps, the stones used in the railings and elsewhere all employ the "greatest" yang or odd number, that is, the number 9 or its multiples.

圜丘北欞門　The north gate of the Circular Mound.

七星石　相傳是天上掉下的隕石，石上有雲紋，實爲人造，以此表示天象。

Qixingshi (Seven Star Stones). They were traditionally believed to be meteors, but are actually man-made objects symbolizing natural phenomena.

九龍柏　樹幹扭結糾纏，恰似九龍盤旋，故名九龍柏。

Nine-Dragon Cypress. The tree is so knotted that it seems entwined by dragons.

雙環亭　兩個圓亭套　Double-ring Tower.
合一起，造型別緻。

大　觀　園
Daguanyuan

位於北京城西南隅的護城河畔，它是八十年代中期依據中國著名古典小說《紅樓夢》描述的場景而建造的，是一座典型的清代官家園林。《紅樓夢》主要通過賈寶玉、林黛玉、薛寶釵三人間的愛情糾葛及其不幸結局，反映了十八世紀中國封建貴族的興衰史。大觀園再現了小說中描寫的庭院樓閣、亭臺水榭。遊人漫步園中，不由得見物思情，引發懷古幽思。

Daguanyuan (Grand View Garden), located at the southeastern corner of Beijing, is a newly-built garden. Its hills, ponds and buildings are all based on the classical Chinese novel *A Dream of Red Mansions*. A history of the rise and fall of feudal nobles in the eighteenth century China, the novel vividly describes the love story and tragic fate of Jia Baoyu, Lin Daiyu and Xue Baochai. A visit to the garden will make you reflect on the ancient events.

大觀園　Daguanyuan

省親別墅 由前後兩個庭院組成，是接待皇妃賈元春的行宮。

The House Reunion. Consisting of two large courtyards, this is the temporary palace for the Imperial Consort, Jia Yuanchun.

"顧恩思義"大殿 省親別墅的主要建築。殿堂裝飾富麗堂皇，以顯示皇妃的威嚴氣派。

Palace of "Recalling Imperial Favour, Mindful of Duty". This magnificent palace is the main building of the Grand View Garden.

怡紅院　小説男主人公賈寶玉的住所。垂花門樓裝飾華麗，以示他是達官豪門之後。

The Happy Red Court. This is the living place of Jia Baoyu, the main character of the novel.

"怡紅快綠"　賈寶玉的卧室。室内有四位漂亮丫環的蠟像，既説明貴族少爺的闊綽，又展示了他不拘世俗，甘與下人爲伍的叛逆性格。

Chamber of "Happy Red and Delightful Green". This is Jia Baoyu's bedroom, with four beautiful wax-maids standing in it. This symbolizes not only Jia Baoyu's nobility but also the rebellious nature which leads him to break the feudal ethical code and befriend lower-class people.

怡紅院長廊　長廊貼金彩繪，裝飾華麗，漫步其中，如履畫廊。

The corridor of the Happy Red Court. Decorated with paintings, this corridor is very magnificent.

瀟湘館　小説女主人公林黛玉的住所。建築以淡
緑色爲主調，以突出房主人寄人籬下，内心悲苦而又
孤傲自許的心態。

Xiaoxiang Lodge.　This is the courtyard of Lin Daiyu, the
main heroine of the novel. To bring out her character, her
living quarters are decorated with pale green bamboo designs.

蘅蕪院　小説另一女主人公薛寶釵的住所。院内以嶙峋怪石作點綴，以展示這位大家閨秀莊重嚴謹的性格。

The Alpinia Park. This is the place where Xue Baochai, another heroine of the novel, lives. The grotesquely-shaped rocks in the courtyard symbolize the serious, solemn nature of the girl from the nobility.

稻香村　這裏有竹籬茅舍，果樹稻田，水井酒幌，呈現的是山村野趣，田園風光。

The Paddy-Sweet Cottage. This thatched hut with a bamboo fence, fruit trees, paddy-field, a well and wine-shop sign around it represents a rural scene.

滴翠亭 依照小説中"寶釵戲彩蝶"的故事而建造
的湖心亭。在這裏可聞水聲，可觀湖景，亦可品茗抒
情。

Dripping Emerald Pavilion. This lake pavilion is based on
the story of Xue Baochai chasing a butterfly. Visitors can hear
the sound of dripping water, enjoy the lake scene and write
poems.

藕香榭　臨水而建的長亭。遊人至此，可見魚戲荷動，垂柳
倒映的趣景。

Lotus Fragrance Anchorage.　From this pavilion visitors can enjoy fish
swimming among the lotus and reflections of hanging willow trees in the lake.

沁芳亭　亭臺濱湖而建，湖岸廣植花木。登亭憩息，柳清花香，令人心曠神怡。

Refreshing Fragrant Pavilion. Surrounded by flowers and trees, this lakeside pavilion is a very refreshing place.

長　城

The Great Wall

中國古代重要的軍事設施。始建於公元前七世紀。秦始皇統一中國後，爲防止北方匈奴貴族南侵，於公元前二一四年開始將各諸侯國建造的長城予以修復、增築、連接，歷時十年，構成龐大的整體。以後，歷代王朝都根據自己的防禦需要，加以重修。到了明代，前後修築長城十八次，歷時約二百年，使它西起甘肅省的嘉峪關，東至河北省的山海關，越羣山，過草地，穿沙漠，橫跨六省一市，總長達六千七百餘公里，大部分至今基本完好。北京八達嶺長城是明長城的代表。城墻高八點五米，厚六點五米，頂寬五點七米，女墻高一米，蜿蜒曲折，氣勢非凡，實爲世界一大奇觀。

The Great Wall is a gigantic defensive project whose beginning can be traced as far back as the 7th century B.C. After Qin Shihuang (the First Emperor of the Qin) (245-209 B.C.) unified China, he began in 214 B.C. to connect and extend the fortifications which the rival feudal kingdoms had built around their territories for self-protection, with the purpose to guard against invasion by nomadic tribes to the north. It took ten years to complete the project.

Subsequent dynasties continued to strengthen and extend the wall according to the needs of their own defence. In the Ming Dynasty 18 large-scale reconstructions were carried out, and it took about two hundred years to complete the Great Wall. Starting from Jiayuguan in Gansu Province in the west, it runs through mountains, grasslands and deserts, passes through six provinces and one municipality and finally reaches into the sea at Shanhaiguan in Hebei in the east, covering 6,700 kilometres. Most of the Ming Great Wall remains in reasonably good condition today. It is 8.5 metres high, 6.5 metres wide at the base and 5.7 metres wide at the top, with a parapet of 1 metre high. The Great Wall is known as one of the world's wonders.

長　城　The Great Wall

　　居庸關雲臺　居庸關爲北京北面的門户，長城的重要關口之一。雲臺是居庸關的著名景點。這裏層巒叠嶂，花木葱鬱，是燕京八景之一，被稱爲"居庸叠翠"。

Juyongguan, Beijing's northern door, is one of the most important passes of the Great Wall. Yuntai is a famous scenic spot in Juyongguan. High mountain peaks rise one after another and are covered with wild flowers and undergrowth. It used to be one of the famous "Eight Views of Yanjing" here.

券門觀景
On the Great Wall.

長城瑞雪
The Great Wall in the snow.

長城秋色
Autumn scene at the Great Wall.

月下敵樓
Watchtower in the moonlight.

長城夕照

The Great Wall at sunset.

長城晨暉

Morning over the Great Wall.

慕田峪長城　位於北京東北約七十公里處。此段長城墻體完整，空心敵樓別具一格，加之山勢崢嶸，自然環境優美，頗有高山園林的特色。

The Great Wall at Mutianyu. Located 70 kilometres northeast of Beijing, this section of the Great Wall is well preserved too. It has watchtowers of a unique style. The high and precipitous mountains are very beautiful; it looks like a mountain garden.

慕田峪長城障牆
The Great Wall at Mutianyu.

金山嶺長城　此處長城
僅二十五公里就設敵樓一百
四十座，且造型精巧多樣，
有臺形、扁形、圓形的，有
船篷頂、平頂、穹隆頂的，
應有盡有，堪稱明長城的精
粹。

The Great Wall at Jinshanling.
This is yet another prime scenic
spot along the Great Wall near
Beijing. In just 25 kilometres
alone there are 140 watchtowers.
They are cleverly constructed in a
variety of intricate shapes: terrace-
shaped, flat-shaped and round-
shaped watchtowers with sail-like,
flat, or vaulted roofs. Jinshanling
can be said to represent the height
of the Ming Great Wall.

金山嶺長城障牆

The Great Wall at Jinshanling

明 十 三 陵

The Ming Tombs

位於北京西北郊約五十公里處。陵區以長陵所在的天壽山爲主峰，東西羣山迴抱，構成一個天然大庭院，院門開在南端，蟒山、虎峪山雄峙兩側，恰似一龍一虎守護着大門。向南爲遼闊的平原，明代的十三個皇帝就埋在這羣山環繞、松柏掩映的區域內，總面積約四十平方公里。

明十三陵從一四〇九年修建長陵起，至一六四四年修建思陵止，歷時二百餘年，其時，這裏是一片"禁區"，憑添了許多神秘色彩。

一九五六年初夏，中國考古工作者發掘了明萬曆皇帝朱翊鈞的陵墓——定陵，發現了地下宮殿。除棺槨外，出土金銀珠寶、服飾玉器等寶物三千多件，揭開了定陵的秘密。從此明十三陵聲名大振，成爲北京的旅遊勝地。

The Ming Tombs lie at the foot of the Tianshou Mountains, some 50 kilometres northwest of Beijing. Surrounded by hills, the place looks like a natural courtyard, with the Long Dragon Hill and the Crouching Tiger Hill lying on either side of its south entrance. Thirteen Ming emperors were buried here. Covered with ancient pine and cypress trees, this imperial cemetery occupies an area of 40 square kilometres.

The construction of this necropolis continued for over 200 years from the first tomb, the Changling, which began in 1409 to the last one, the Siling, which was built in 1644. During the 200 years this place was a forbidden area.

In the early summer of 1956 Chinese archaeologists began the excavation of the Dingling underground palace, the tomb of the thirteenth emperor, Zhu Yijun (1573-1620). In addition to the underground palace and coffins, more than 3,000 pieces of gold, silver, pearl and cloth were unearthed. From that time on, the Ming Tombs has become widely known as a not-to-be-missed spot for visitors.

明 十 三 陵　The Ming Tombs

神道　道兩邊有十八對石人石獸。石人爲勳臣、文臣和武將，均爲站像；石獸是獅、獬豸（傳說中的怪獸）、駱駝、象、麒麟和馬，姿態各異，或立或臥，是不可多得的石雕藝術珍品。

The Sacred Way. Along both sides of the Sacred Way is an impressive array of 24 stone animals followed by twelve stone human figures. The human figures are military, civil and meritorious officials, and the stone animals are lions, xiezhi (a mythical beast said to know good and evil), camels, elephants, qilin (a mythical unicorn-like beast) and horses, some of which are standing while others are kneeling. All are elegant stone carvings.

石牌坊　十三陵的第一座建築物，夾柱石雕有麒麟和獅子，額枋上是飄逸的雲紋，製作精巧，造型宏偉。

Stone Arch. The first construction of the Ming Tombs, it is exquisitely carved with animals and other designs on its pillars.

碑亭及亭側華表　此亭雙層檐頭，四面開門，內竪龍頂龜趺石碑一座，碑文長達三千五百餘字。

Stele Pavilion and White Marble Pillars. The pavilion has double eaves, with doors open in four directions. Inside the pavilion is a tall stele standing on the back of a stone tortoise with a dragon's head on its top. It bears an inscription of more than 3,500 words.

長陵明樓　明樓是陵墓的標誌。長陵是十三陵始建的第一座陵墓，埋葬着明代第三個皇帝朱棣。站在明樓四望，整個陵區盡收眼底。

Minglou (Soul Tower) of Changling. Minglou is the symbol for a tomb. Changling is the first and biggest tomb, which contains the remains of the third Ming emperor Zhu Di, whose reign lasted from 1403 to 1425. The entire necropolis can be seen from this tower.

長陵祾恩殿　座落在三層白石臺基上，是中國最大的木結構建築。

Ling'endian (Hall of Prominent Favour). This hall stands on a three-tiered marble terrace and is one of the largest wooden buildings in China.

祾恩殿內景　殿內三十二根巨形楠木柱均產自中國西南深山，一根巨木從採伐到運至陵區，需五六年，許多民工爲此喪命。

The interior of Ling'endian. The hall's coffered ceiling is supported by 32 huge gilded pillars of nanmu (a fine hardwood), each made of a single trunk. The timber came from the mountains in southwest China and took five to six years to transport to Beijing.

定陵　是十三陵中的第十座陵墓，埋葬着明代第十三位皇帝朱翊鈞和他的兩個皇后。

Dingling. The tomb of the thirteenth Ming emperor, Zhu Yijun, and his two empresses.

寶城　是一道圓形磚圍墻，設有垛口，周長約七百五十米，圍墻內封土下即是墓室。

Baocheng (Precious Wall). This circular wall around the mound is about 750 metres in circumference with crenels on the top. Beneath the mound is the underground palace where the emperor is buried.

定陵地下宮殿入口

The entrance to the underground palace.

地下宫殿甬道

The passageway of the underground palace.

地宮中殿長明燈　燈油放在青花龍紋大瓷缸
內，地宮封閉時，燈是燃的，因缺氧自滅。

The everlasting lamp in the underground palace. Oil is
contained in a blue-and-white porcelain tub with dragon design, with a bronze bowl with a wick floating on its surface.
The lamp was lit when the tomb was sealed, its flame dying
out for want of oxygen.

定陵棺椁　中間是皇帝朱翊鈞的棺椁，兩側爲皇后的棺椁。

Coffins in Dingling.　The coffin in the middle is the
emperor's, and the ones on the two sides are the empresses'.

出土金冠　全部用金絲編織而成。冠頂上金龍製作精細，形態生動。同時出土的還有皇后戴的鳳冠。這些瑰寶均爲首次發現

Gold crown. This gold crown was the emperor's imperial crown. It is made of very fine gold thread woven into a filigree bonnet and decorated at the back with two dragons. Also unearthed were the phoenix crowns worn by the empresses. They are the first imperial crowns discovered in excavations in China.

鳳冠　The phoenix crown

茂陵雪景　Maoling in the Snow

恭 王 府 花 園

Garden of Prince Gong's Residence

建於十八世紀下半葉，是北京現存較完整的一座王府花園。恭王府原爲清代大學士和珅的私邸。和珅爲官二十年，植黨營私，斂財納賄，招致殺身之禍，被抄没家產，宅邸遂改爲慶王府。一八五一年，咸豐皇帝封奕訢爲恭親王，賜慶王府爲官邸，改名爲恭王府。

奕訢進住後，在府後建樓挖池，堆山植樹，闢爲萃錦園。此園三面環土山，內有竹子院、詩畫舫、戲樓等大小二十景，各景間佈局自然，疏密有致，融北方建築風格與江南造園藝術於一體，堪稱私家古典園林中的佳作。

Built in the later part of the eighteenth century, this is a well-preserved garden of a prince's residence in Beijing. Prince Gong's residence originally was the private residence of He Shen (1750-1799), the Grand Secretary of the Qing Dynasty. In the twenty years he was in office, He Shen formed a clique to pursue selfish interests, accumulate wealth and take bribes. So he was killed and his properties were confiscated, and his residence was changed to the residence of Prince Qing. In 1851 Emperor Xianfeng made Yixin a prince and gave the place to him. It was bestowed upon Prince Gong as his official residence.

After Yixin moved in, he built pavilions, dug ponds, made hills and planted trees in the rear part of the residence, turning it into a garden. Surrounded by hills on three sides, the garden has twenty scenic spots of different sizes such as the Bamboo Courtyard, Pavilion for Poetry and Painting and the Theatre. Well arranged and exquisitely constructed, the garden combines the architectural style of north China with the art of the garden of south China; it is a fine example of an antique private garden.

恭王府花園　*Garden of Prince Gong's Residence*

獨樂峰　奕訢自持
天潢貴胄，將"獨"字
刻於石頂，石因此得名。

Dulefeng (Peak of
Unique Joy). Yixin regard-
ed himself as supremely no-
ble, so he had the character
"Unique" carved at the top
of the rock.

竹子院　院内以翠
竹爲主，花木爲輔，以
表房主的清高雅趣。

Bamboo Courtyard. The
courtyard is full of green
bamboo, plants and flowers.
It showed the loftiness of its
owner.

詩畫舫　建於池塘
中心，非乘舟不得登
亭，別有一番新意。

Pavilion for Poetry and Painting.　Built in the centre of a
pond, it can be reached only by boat. The architectural idea is
very novel.

　　戲樓　實爲一層封閉大殿，酷似現代劇場。據考證，此類戲樓，在清代極少見。

The Theatre. This theatre is a one-storeyed close hall much like a modern theatre. According to textual research, theatre of this kind was very rare in the Qing Dynasty.

　　戲樓內景　望樓懸掛"壽"燈，四壁貼花彩繪，臺上演戲，臺下品茗，頗有"春夜宴桃園"的意趣。

The interior of the theatre. Many "longevity" lanterns are hung on the stage, and the walls are decorated with paintings. The audience can drink tea while enjoying the performance.

庭院一角　這裏花木茂盛，建築精美，環境幽静。

A corner of the garden. Surrounded by flowers and trees, the buildings are very elegant and the environment is quiet.

榆關　石碑上刻有"翠雲嶺"，關口雖小，卻是仿長城而造。

Yuguan (Elm Pass). On the stone tablet is carved "Purple Cloud Range". The pass, though small, is an imitation of the Great Wall.

圓 明 園 遺 址

The Ruins of Yuanmingyuan

圓明園是環繞福海的圓明、萬春、長春三園之總稱。始建於一七○九年，歷時一百五十年陸續建成。清王朝傾全國物力，征集無數能工巧匠，鑿湖堆山，種植奇花異木，集國內外名勝四十景，建成大型建築物一百四十五處，內收難以計數的藝術珍品和圖書文物。在這些建築中，除具有中國風格的庭院外，長春園內還有海晏堂、遠瀛觀等西洋風格的建築羣，並利用長廊、墻垣、橋樑與自然景物相映襯，藝術價值甚高，被譽爲"萬園之園"。

遺憾的是，這一園林藝術傑作，分別於一八六○年、一九○○年遭英法聯軍、八國聯軍的劫掠和焚燒，遂使一代名園化爲廢墟。現在，經整修後的遺址，已成爲人民羣衆憑吊和遊覽的場所。

Yuanmingyuan was a large imperial park. It was actually three separate parks: Yuanmingyuan (Park of Perfection and Brightness), Wanchunyuan (Park of Ten Thousand Springs) and Changchunyuan (Park of Everlasting Spring), centred around the lake, Fuhai (Sea of Happiness). Its construction started in 1709 and took 150 years to complete. The Qing Dynasty assembled the best building materials and employed armies of skilled builders who dug lakes, made hills and planted rare trees and flowers, constructing 40 scenic spots and 145 large buildings, some of which contained valuable art treasures and libraries. Among these buildings, most of them were in the Chinese courtyard style, but some were Western in style. Against the site of great natural beauty, the various groups of buildings were connected by long corridors, walls and bridges and embodied the most refined techniques of Chinese art and architecture. So Yuanmingyuan was known as "the park of parks".

Unfortunately, in 1860 the Anglo-French joint forces invaded Beijing, looted all the treasures in the park and set fire to it, thus reducing this famous creation to smouldering ruins. In 1900 the allied forces of the Eight Powers invaded Beijing and sacked the remaining buildings in the park. Today, the ruins of Yuanmingyuan are protected, and it has become a place for people to visit and ponder on the past.

圓 明 園 遺 址
The Ruins of Yuanmingyuan

西洋樓殘迹
Ruins of the Western-style buildings.

　　福海　是圓明園中最大的人工湖,湖心原有仙境般
的"蓬島瑤臺"。這是整修後的福海景色。

　　Fuhai (Sea of Happiness). This was the largest man-made
lake in Yuanmingyuan. Originally, in the middle of the lake
was an island called the Fairy Isle and Jade Terrace. This is the
restored Fuhai.

紫碧山房遺址　這裏是全園的最高點，原來殿宇輝煌，登高可覽全園，現在僅存碎石荒草。

Ruins of Zibishanfang (Purple and Azure Mountain Hall). This is the highest place in the park. Originally a magnificent hall, now it is only broken stones and wild grass.

西峰秀色　原爲四十景之一，現在一片狼藉，面目全非。

Ruins of Xifengxiuse (Beautiful West Peak). Originally it was one of the forty scenic spots here, but now it is nothing but ruins.

方外觀遺址　原爲豪華的西式建築，相傳是乾隆皇帝的寵妃香妃（維吾爾女子，傳其身體有異香，故得名）的寢宮。

Ruins of Fangwaiguan. Originally there was a Western-style building here which was said to be the palace of Emperor Qianlong's favourite concubine Xiangfei, a Uygur girl. She was said to have a special kind of fragrance on her body. That was why she was called Xiangfei (Fragrant Concubine).

雍和宮

Yonghegong Lamasery

北京最大的喇嘛廟。位於城區東北安定門内，建於一六九四年，原爲清雍正皇帝爲皇子時居住的府邸，稱雍親王府，一七二五年改名雍和宮，後改建爲喇嘛廟。

雍和宮由三座牌坊和天王殿、雍和宮大殿、永佑殿、法輪殿、萬福閣等五進建築組成，另有東西配殿和四學殿。整個建築巍峨壯麗，並兼有漢、滿、蒙、藏民族特色。各殿供有衆多佛像，還有大量珍貴文物，其中「五百羅漢山」、金絲楠木佛龕和十八米高的檀木大佛最負盛名，被稱爲雍和宮的「三絶」。

Yonghegong (Palace of Harmony and Peace), the largest lamasery in Beijing, is located inside Andingmen in the city's East District. Built in 1694, the lamasery was originally the residence of the Yongzheng emperor before he ascended the throne. In 1725 it was renamed Yonghegong and declared a lama temple.

Yonghegong consists of three archways, five main halls — Tianwangdian (Devaraja Hall), Yonghedian (Hall of Harmony and Peace), Yongyoudian (Hall of Everlasting Protection), Falundian (Hall of the Dharma Wheel) and Wanfuge (Pavilion of Ten Thousand Happiness) — and the east and west side halls and the "Four Study Halls". These magnificent buildings possess the architectural features of the Han, Man, Mongolian and Tibetan nationalities. The statues of Buddhas in the halls are lifelike. Among the large number of cultural relics preserved in the lamasery, the most important objects are the elaborate "Mountain of Five Hundred Arhats", the 18-metre high sandalwood Buddha and the big shrine made of *nanmu* (a fine hardwood).

雍和宮法輪殿

Yonghegong Lamasery

雍和宮大門前的牌樓
The archway in front of the temple's main entrance.

雍和門　又名天王殿，原爲雍親王府大門。殿內匾書和對聯是乾隆皇帝的御筆。

Yonghemen or the Devaraja Hall, formerly the entrance of Yongzheng's residence. The couplet and the inscriptions on the board were written by Emperor Qianlong.

布袋僧　俗稱彌勒佛，供于天王殿內。

The statue of Maitreya in the Devaraja Hall.

　　韋馱像　佛教守護神之一，又稱韋天將軍。他手持寶杵，面北立于天王殿後門。

Veda with a vajra (mace) in hand stands facing the north at the back door of the Devaraja Hall.

萬福閣 大殿爲木結構，内供十八米高的檀木大佛。

Wanfuge (Pavilion of Ten Thousand Happiness). This pavilion has a wooden structure, and inside it is the 18-metre high statue of Buddha carved from sandalwood.

御碑亭 碑文用滿、漢、蒙、藏四種文字書寫，所以又叫做四體文碑亭。

Yubeiting (Pavilion of the Imperial Stele). In the pavilion is a stele inscribed in Han, Manchu, Mongolian and Tibetan, so it is also called the Pavilion of the Four-language Stele.

邁達拉佛　由一根直徑三米
的巨形檀木雕成，地上十八米，
地下還有八米，爲雍和宮"三絕"
之一。

The statue of Maitreya. Carved from
a single trunk of white sandalwood,
three metres in diameter, the statue
rises 18 metres above ground and sinks
8 metres below. It is one of the "Three
Wonders" in the temple.

旃檀佛　供於照佛樓，其佛龕和火焰背光係楠
木雕成，爲雍和宮"三絕"之一。

The Sandalwood Buddha. The statue of Buddha stands in
Zhaofulou (Tower of the Shining Buddha), and the throne is
carved out of nanmu (a fine hardwood). This fine carving is
also one of the "Three Wonders" in the temple.

十八羅漢　供于雍和宮大殿內。

The Eighteen Arhats in the Hall of Harmony and Peace.

五百羅漢山　　山用檀香木精雕而成，五百羅漢用
金、銀、銅、鐵、錫五種金屬製成，是一組極為珍貴
的藝術品，雍和宮"三絕"之一。

The Mountain of Five Hundred Arhats. The mountain is
carved out of red sandalwood, and the arhats are modelled out
of five metals (gold, silver, bronze, iron and tin). This rare
piece of art is also one of the "Three Wonders" in the temple.

大　鐘　寺

Dazhongsi

座落在北京北三環西路。原名覺生寺，建於清雍正十一年（1733年），因寺內藏有一口明永樂年間鑄造的大鐘，俗稱"大鐘寺"。

這裏已闢爲收藏、研究、展覽各類古鐘的博物館。內有大鐘樓、鐘林館、藏經樓、古鐘鑄造工藝和永樂大鐘銘文陳列室等處。共收入大小古鐘數百件，以供遊人參觀。

Dazhongsi (Great Bell Temple) is situated to the north of the Third Ring Road in the northwestern suburbs of Beijing. Built in 1733 in the reign of the Yongzheng emperor of the Qing Dynasty, its original name was Jueshengsi (Temple of Awakening). Since the famous great bell it houses was brought here in 1743, it has popularly been known as Dazhongsi.

Today, Dazhongsi has become a museum to collect, study and display various kinds of ancient bells. Inside it there are the Big Bell Tower, the Bell Hall, the Sutra Hall and Exhibition Hall as well as a collection of several hundred ancient bells.

大鐘寺山門　Dazhongsi

華嚴覺海

鐘樓　大鐘寺獨具特色的核心建築，聳立在巨大的青石基上，樓形上圓下方，象徵"天圓地方"。

The Bell Tower. This unique tower is the centre of the Great Bell Temple. Built on an huge base, it is round at the top and square at the bottom, symbolizing that the sky is round and the earth is square.

永樂大鐘　通高六點
七　五米，最大直徑三點
三米，重達四點六五萬公
斤。

The Yongle Bell. The bell is
6.75 metres high and weighs
46.5 tons. The outer rim of the
lip measures 3.3 metres in diameter. It is known as the King
of Bells.

鐘林　其中最古的鐘是宋代熙寧年
間（公元 1068-1078 年）鑄造的，距今九
百余 年，最晚者爲清末鑄造，亦有百年。

Bells. The earliest bell among these is
900 years old, made in the Xining Period
(1068-1078) of the Song Dynasty, and the
latest is over 100 years old, made in the
later part of the Qing Dynasty.

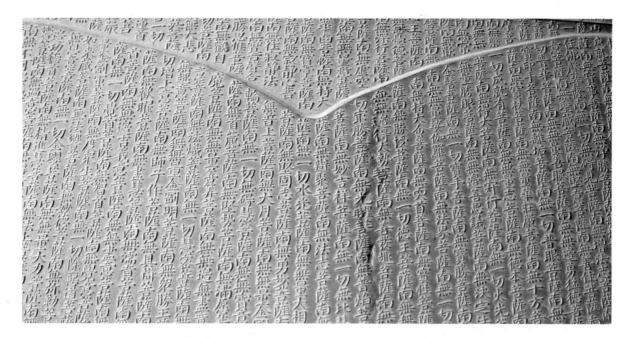

大鐘銘文　鐘體上鑄有漢文經咒十六種，梵文咒語一百余種，共二十三萬余字。

Inscriptions on the Great Bell. The bell is cast with 16 sutras in Chinese and over 100 sutras in Sanskrit on it, totalling 230,000 characters.

朝鐘 　此鐘造型極美觀，鐘壁蛟龍栩栩如生。鐘體未鑄款識，僅在鐘唇上鑄有八個
"☰"，這是八卦中的"乾"卦，加上鐘壁上的蛟龍，"龍""隆"諸音，可推測爲乾隆年間鑄
造。

The Chao Bell. This is a beautifully-shaped bell, with lifelike dragons cast on it. It has no inscriptions
of the time it was made. But according to its design, it is believed to have been made in the Qianlong
Period of the Qing.

香　山

Xiangshan Park

　　位於北京西北約四十公里處的西山東麓，其最高峰爲香爐峰，因峰頂有兩塊巨石，形似"香鼎"，故名香山。這裏風景名勝甚多，其中尤以香山公園的見心齋、雙清別墅、琉璃塔以及與公園爲鄰的碧雲寺和臥佛寺爲最佳。

　　香山公園是一座典型的森林公園。園林清幽，景色迷人，特別在深秋時節，遍山的黃櫨樹呈現出"霜葉紅於二月花"的動人景象。西山賞秋觀紅葉已成爲北京人一年一度的盛會。

　　碧雲寺與香山公園毗鄰。此寺採用層層封閉的建築手法。從山門至寺頂，共六層，迴旋串連，給人以層出不窮之感。寺內以五百羅漢堂和金剛寶座塔最負盛名。

　　臥佛寺距香山公園約二公里。全稱"十方普覺寺"，因寺內有臥佛造像，俗稱臥佛寺。此寺建在一條南北中綫上，前立彩坊，背負青山，中間四重殿院，層層深入，一氣貫通。兩旁配襯着廊廡別院，給人以主體建築突出，羣房殿堂生輝的感覺。

Xiangshan (Fragrance Hill) Park is located on the eastern side of the Western Hills about 40 kilometres to the northwest of Beijing. On top of the hill, 557 metres above sea level, are two huge rocks, which are shaped like incense-burning tripods. Hence the name of the hill.

Inside the park there are many scenic spots, the famous ones being Jianxinzhai (Pavilion of Revealing One's Mind), Shuangqing (Twin Clear Waters), Liulita (Glazed Tile Pagoda) and the nearby Biyunsi (Temple of Azure Clouds) and Wofosi (Temple of the Recumbent Buddha).

Xiangshan is a typical forest park. The sceneries are very beautiful, especially in late autumn when the tree leaves turn red. Every year Beijing people come here to enjoy the red leaves.

Biyunsi is close to Xiangshan Park. The temple is constructed on six different levels from the entrance gate to the pagoda at the summit, and has a series of interconnecting courtyards, each with its own special character. The Five Hundred Arhats and the Diamond Throne Pagoda are the most famous features in the temple.

Two kilometres away from Xiangshan Park lies Wofosi, whose full name is Shifang Pujuesi (Temple of Universal Awakening). It is better known as Wofosi because it has a statue of a recumbent Buddha. The buildings in this temple have a unique style; they are built along a central line, with a painted archway standing in the front, a green hill in the rear, and four courtyards running one after another from the front to the back flanked by small courtyards. With great architectural value, the temple is very impressive.

見心齋　具有江南園林風格的別緻庭院。院心有半圓水池，齋房臨水而立，環境極爲幽静。

Jianxinzhai (Pavilion of Revealing One's Mind). This is an exquisite small courtyard in the style of a southern Chinese garden. In the centre of the small courtyard is a semicircular pond, by which side stands the pavilion. It is known as "a park within a park".

雙清別墅　位於半坡的寧靜小院，內有荷池，兩股清泉自石縫流入池中，故名"雙清"。

Shuangqing (Twin Clear Waters). Half way up the hill lies a small quiet courtyard with a lotus pool in it. The pool is fed by two springs, named Shuangqing (Twin Clear Waters).

香山飯店　近年興建的現代化旅遊飯店，設備先進，環境優美。

Xiangshan Hotel. A recently-built modern hotel with advanced facilities and a beautiful natural environment.

香　山　Xiangshan Park

琉璃塔　七層八角式塔，八角檐端綴
有銅鈴，微風拂過，叮噹作響。

The Glazed-Tile Pagoda. Octagonal and seven-storeyed, the pagoda has 56 bronze bells dangling from its eaves.

碧雲寺牌樓　　**Archway of Biyunsi.**

碧雲寺金剛寶座塔　全部用漢白玉石砌成，上面
布滿精緻的浮雕，造型極爲華美。

The Diamond Throne Pagoda in Biyunsi. Constructed out
of white marble, the whole building is covered with exquisite
relief carvings and represents a high level of architectural skill.

羅漢堂　內有羅漢像五百零八尊，均爲硬木雕成，
外飾金箔。羅漢像姿態各異，神情有別，係藝術珍品。

The Hall of Arhats. All together there are 508 arhats carved
out of hardwood and decorated in gold foil. Each of them is
portrayed in a different pose and with a different expression.

卧佛寺琉璃坊

The glazed-tile archway in Wofosi.

　　卧佛　銅質，鑄造於一三二一年，長五米多，重
約五十四噸，是罕見的歷史文物。

　　Statue of the Recumbent Buddha. Cast out of copper in
1321, the statue weighs about 54 tons and is more than 5
metres in length.

編　輯	望天星	
翻　譯	熊振儒	
攝　影	曲維波	任詩吟
	劉思功	姜景余
	羅文發	高明義
	劉啓俊	黃韜朋
	牛嵩林	董宗貴
	趙明清	王春澍
	杜澤泉	蒙　紫
	劉春根	張肇基
	孫樹明	胡維標
	于天爲	徐　訊

装幀設計　李士伋

北京風景集萃

*

中國世界語出版社出版

北京一二○一廠印制

中國國際圖書貿易總公司發行

(中國北京車公莊西路 35 號)

北京郵政信箱第 399 號　郵政編碼 100044

1994 年(16 開)第二版第五次印刷

ISBN 7-5052-0043-7／K · 9(外)

04500

85-CE-362P